NLP

Discover The Power Of Neuro-Linguistic Programming
And Hypnosis For Immediate People Liking You: Master
The Art Of Instant People Liking You Through The Use Of
Hypnosis, NLP, And Persuasion

Jean-Pierre Morin

TABLE OF CONTENT

NLP Foundations 1

Handling Trauma And Phobias 11

What Is NLP Darkness? 28

Neuro-Linguistic Programming: What Is It? 66

Why Visualization Is Effective—As Is All Of Nlp. 81

Why People Who Manipulate Do So 103

Neuro-Linguistic Programming Techniques 141

How Should Your Goals Be Formulated? 159

NLP Foundations

Human habits are shaped by behavioural patterns and behaviours, according to NLP. Taking charge of one's life is possible if one knows their routines, patterns, and behaviours. NLP covers a vast range of topics, but in essence, it's about our motivations and the reasons behind our choices. They're also known as metaprograms.

How do Metaprograms work?
Different mental disorders are guided, managed, and identified by the mental process. It also establishes other cognitively demanding activities. The

word comes from a term used in computer science. Additionally, it alludes to how computer programs operate. When reduced to its most basic form, the term signifies programs, which are the instructions needed to operate a computer or PC, and meta, which is a higher level.

The major and principal programs, called built-in behaviours, are metaprograms. Additionally, they control other computer programs, and that's usually how you think. In the field of NLP, there are numerous metaprograms. When utilized on the internet, the five listed will have variances.

Metaprograms have two dimensions; no one version fits all people perfectly. Additionally, some people fit on both versions. This is because they explain how individuals might be categorized and the causes behind their actions. They also don't intend to distinguish between a person's conduct and traits. The most popular metaprograms determine who the mind functions for, demonstrate how the mind functions, and evaluate the conduct in question.

It deals with both similarity and diversity.

The sameness version looks for activities that are comfortable for them and is always driven by similar things. They are aware of similarities. They end up liking what they seek because they feel confident in what they want. In addition, every scenario from earlier encounters. And it benefits them when it is done again.

However, variations in versions always reveal differences in things. They welcome change, are eager to learn new things, and always try new things. They search for irregularities and make swift changes when they find them. Even when unnecessary, they have an insatiable desire to alter everything. By recognizing and comprehending the contrasts, they can recognize and comprehend possibilities.

Moving aside and in the direction of something

To put it plainly, the prospect of achieving their goals motivates most people with these attributes. Reaching their goals gives them joy and fulfilment. Setting objectives is what drives them because it's something they can do often and with ease. Their will to succeed drives them to cross tasks off their to-do list. This ultimately leaves them with a sense of fulfilment.

By the other ones, they imply that their only concern is getting away from any discomfort or potential danger. Their inclination stems from their capacity to avoid conflict. They think they are secure and at ease. Before doing any action, they are free of any challenges and difficulties.

both indoors and outside

The internal group always establishes the standards. They establish criteria that enable them to feel confident in receiving approval and making choices. They don't seek proof that they made the right choice or performed well. They always feel they have fulfilled their expectations and aspirations when they accomplish anything well. When given too much knowledge, they become demotivated and always require room to reach their objectives.

Those using the external version rely on others for standards, guidelines, and permission. They always enjoy receiving a pat on the back for anything they accomplish and prefer to be controlled and observed. This gesture gives them a sense of recognition, approval, and appreciation. They are always unmotivated and unsure of their talents when they don't receive feedback.

The steps involved and available options
When people are presented with a comprehensive overview of all the possibilities, they always search for the one that best suits their needs. They like more options and are not interested in finer specifics. They can choose to delve further into their own identities.

When responses are given, those involved always put forth much effort. They make sure everything is done correctly and arrange all the necessary details. They constantly wish they could access all knowledge, such as routines and structures that make their work easier.

Proactive is what is reactive.

They are called initiators in the case of the proactive variant. They never hesitate to complete their assignments on their own. They don't think much about what will happen in the future; they are just focused on the here and now. They are always focused on the tangible and the idea that everything should be true. They are always focused on their tasks, whether they are completed or still to be completed.

The reactive person usually plans and spends much time observing their surroundings. Every choice they make must go through a carefully thought-out, preplanned process. They set their deadlines and commit to knowing what needs to be done. Their attention is always on scheduling and what to access. And constantly waiting for the ideal moment to get ready and complete a task.

Sometimes, most people will have a combination of versions and patterns. Some, however, err on the side of greater bias. Despite this, NLP metaprograms are fascinating because they penetrate the human psyche and help people comprehend themselves. People can better comprehend and improve upon one another as a result of diversity. They consistently learn about the behaviours and personal preferences of others.

Furthermore, it forges new connections. NLP assists in taking complete control of the mind and also explains how the mind works, which makes it efficient when operating and consistently promotes the development of a positive mental attitude. Put a lot of effort into their responsibilities.

Handling Trauma And Phobias

A meme, or a brief thinking pattern that we are either given or generate on our own, is necessary for the code of a single event to be assigned to a phobia or trauma.

One Sunday morning, for instance, I was travelling along the M6 when I had to move into the centre lane to pass a little car in the nearby lane. A bus behind me also departed to pass by the same car. The car suddenly shifts sharply to the right, squarely in my path. It is ahead of me by roughly thirty feet or ten meters. My speed is 70 m.p.h., or roughly 100 feet per second, and there is no way I can escape getting into an accident. The other car's back wheel had come off for the record.

Neither the other automobile nor the bus suffered any injuries in the incident with us.

"I am very lucky, someone is looking after me," was all I could think. A driving-related meme to enjoy. "I could have been killed," is what I could have told myself. That idea could have been a meme that led to a motorway fear.

We must unplug the meme and the event to remove the program. There are numerous methods to do this. If it's a straightforward phobia, with just one meme endorsing it, we may easily alter the emotions using a simple method.

Indeed, it is possible to swiftly alter any occurrence linked to a single originating meme.
How can a basic phobia be distinguished from a complicated one? In this context, "complex" refers to a collection of programs with related memes that we could classify as beliefs.

"Sorry, I can't use the lift; I've been scared of lifts ever since I got stuck in one" might be a basic description of a lift phobia. "Sorry, I can't go into that part of town because too many buildings have lifts in them" could be a complex lift phobia. An example of a basic fear of lightning would be, "Thunderstorms terrify me to no end." "I hate thunderstorms, so I check the weather forecast to see if any are likely" might be an example of a complex phobia of lightning.

Phobias can be deeply emotional, often to the point of becoming overwhelming. When such emotions surface while trying to better yourself, STOP and try again later.

I advise creating a strong, secure bail-out anchor if you are a therapist and wish to use this with clients. Start with number five while working on yourself; you won't likely need the anchors.

1. Ask the patient to recall and re-enter when they feel safe and secure to establish a secure bale-out anchor. Ask them to hold your hand; the harder they squeeze, the safer they feel. (In any case, it's a natural reaction, and the hand squeeze helps you be mindful when they shoot the anchor for themselves.)

2. Disrupt the state.

3. Hold their hand as you ask them to feel a little bit of the anxiety so you can identify the phobic reaction.

4. Disrupt state.

5. Ask them to visualize themselves seeing a black-and-white image of their

younger selves in a movie theatre right before the phobic incident. Touch an elbow to secure this posture.

6. Ask them to visualize leaving their body and entering the projection room so they can see the younger version of themselves staring at them from the seat. I utilize my shoulder as an alternative anchor for this position.

You now own three anchors. A projection room, a movie seat, and a bale-out.) To be able to do this, you will need to sit next to the subject.

7. Have them run the black-and-white film from their location in the projection room while they observe themselves in the movie theatre. Make them announce the end of the phobic event and halt the

film. I get them to close their eyes and nod their heads.

8. Ask them to stand within the picture and bring it closer. Then, at your signal, have them run the picture backwards in colour as quickly as possible. Add some clown music if you think it's fitting. Clown music would certainly come across as disrespectful or callous if you were working with a victim of a major attack.

9. Ask them to repeat steps seven and eight five or six times.

10. Send a message to your younger self from your present self, telling it that you love and value it.

11. Ask the future version of yourself to return and express gratitude to the

current version of yourself for the improvements.

12. Allow the three selves to unite and realize their interconnectedness.

13. Optional: Make a movie showing an alternate version of what happened.

The double separation from the unpleasant experience lessens the strength of feelings.

Use the earliest memory of the phobic reaction for phobias and the memory of the incident for traumas.

Simply pausing and returning to the movie will typically be sufficient to ease everyday stress.

Mind maps and neuro-linguistic programming

We now need to examine a new subject: mapping our reality. Everyone's perception of anything will differ greatly from what other people view. A set of twins can have disparate life perspectives. It is more likely that two individuals with disparate theological and geographic backgrounds will arrive with differing perspectives. Nonetheless, individuals from seemingly identical backgrounds may arrive with distinct viewpoints on their interpretation of reality, which sometimes surprises many people.

Social influences will greatly impact how each person behaves and grows. The background of others can impact each person in the community. People in a community, for instance, who all come from more affluent families, will often share a similar worldview. After that, these different points of view would combine to support that region's development and overall operation. It can now also go in the opposite direction. People's lifestyles will probably impact others nearby if there is a particular location where more people commit crimes. There won't be exceptions, and it's not appropriate for everyone. But their mentality will also be greatly influenced by the place they think. Our biological constitution is another factor that can alter the reality we perceive in our imaginations. Anxiety and depression in the family will have a direct impact on a person's personality and even how they interact with others.

Beyond merely the structure of our brains, biological factors are crucial to mapping our experience. You also need to consider the person's views, way of thinking, personality, and mental genetics, including eye colour, skin tone, hair type, and more. There will be disagreement over whether nature or nurture has a greater role. Though individual differences may exist, this is probably a fantastic combination of both. An individual's behaviour and thoughts can be influenced by their upbringing and the people in their immediate environment during all phases of their life.

Interpretation Is Highly Personal

Our experiences differ so greatly from one another that meaning will also change. Many believe that serving a greater power, like God, is the only thing that matters. Some people can interpret this phrase as suggesting that they should pursue happiness. Then, many people believe that life has no purpose at all; whether or not this is true is a matter of opinion. Our personality traits, animalistic actions, genetic makeup, and social upbringing will ultimately define our meaning.

A portion of the issue with our worldview is this. Because meaning can change at any time, it can be subjective. Even if someone believes in God their entire life, they may eventually become an atheist due to events in their lives. Of course, the opposite is also possible. Numerous accounts abound of people who, after believing that they would never be able to acquire faith, do so and go on to become among the most fervent believers in the world.

While we're talking about it, religion is a complex subject because no one is born with a set of beliefs. Although they may have always had a deep sense of personal spirituality, they were taught the concepts associated with Buddhism, Islam, and Christianity. Although meaning is given to us in a particular way, we can explore and develop our definitions and meanings.

While everyone has different thoughts about what they believe to be the most important things in life, sometimes the meaning of life cannot be precisely stated for anyone. If they don't, it eventually impacts their emotions and behaviour. You will discover, though, that there is strength in knowing that, despite your current beliefs, you are free to change them at any moment, no matter how strongly you feel about them. Many people become trapped in one item for an extended period because they are unaware they have this kind of freedom.

These days, NLP procedures assist everyone in realizing this type of inner power, which they may then harness to effect change in their lives. By using effective NLP techniques, a person may examine themselves, identify the issues in their lives, and alter their outlook on everything. Everyone can attempt this, albeit some people will find it more difficult to do so than others.

Because meaning is so individualized, changing other people's opinions or perspectives might occasionally be convenient. Many people are so mired in their beliefs that it is simpler for them to give up on the work necessary to sort things out and cling to whatever insights others may share. It can be riskier for a manipulator to get control over someone when they are unable to reason out their reality or come to their conclusions. Because they have learnt how to implant diverse concepts in the brain, some people who utilize NLP techniques use them to exploit others.

They can locate their victim and manipulate other people's emotions by offering what they are hiding as a fix for the issue that the victim or the lost person is experiencing. Although it may appear that the manipulator is attempting to assist and prioritize the victim's interests, in actuality, this is a ruse to obtain what they desire or move closer to achieving one of their own objectives.

What Is NLP Darkness?

A fascination with corpses

These are the ones who seem attracted to dead bodies sexually. Necrophiliacs' psychological and emotional growth is interrupted because they struggle to form emotional or social ties with others. As they go along the Dark Continuum, their attraction to the inanimateness of corpses grows.

Selfishness

Many people view narcissists and others who possess this trait as those who genuinely "Love Themselves." While this is a good start, it is not precise enough when examining narcissism through the prism of the triad. Being a self-loving person without being a narcissist is very possible. What are some of the differences between a highly shallow person and someone who exhibits enough narcissism to be classified as belonging to The Dark Triad?

When someone fits the scientific diagnostic criteria for narcissism to the extent that they are thought to have a psychological illness, they are likely to consistently display several of the following personality traits. An excessive sense of self-importance is common in narcissists, who may believe that their existence is unique and among the most significant in history. They believe that narcissists are more than just unique; they are sophisticated. They belong to a higher species and are considered superior to "everyday" people. Their actions are a reflection of their confidence.

One of the most prevalent external signs of narcissism is an inability to take any kind of criticism or disagreement. The urge to be flattered is similar to this need to be agreed with. Narcissists live their lives in a way that makes it easy for them to be accepted by others who satisfy their need for constant affirmation, reputation, and praise.

Narcissistic Behavior

Dreams and visions of extreme power and prestige are among the first indications and symptoms of a narcissist. A lot of narcissists harbour aspirations of being liked and worshipped during their formative years. A narcissist will naively believe they deserve this reward and elevation as a basic right, although many non-narcissistic people may also occasionally dream of power and position. The fact that they are no longer universally revered and admired is a personal jab to a psychopath's worldview.

Major narcissists frequently have the conscious belief that "I'm better than a quite number of people, they are no longer worthy of me, and I am better than them." Because of their accomplishments and actions in life, the general public's sense of pride and self-worth fluctuates. The situation with narcissists isn't always like this. Narcissists believe that rewards and flattery are things that they should always automatically obtain, regardless of other options.

The desire for approval and praise, as well as a strong dislike of criticism or rejection, are external behaviours that are a result of the exaggerated sense of self-confidence that narcissists experience on the inside. Praise and a settlement are like air for the selfish ego, whereas criticism and disapproval are poisonous.

Imagine a tyrant in a remote country to get an idea of what narcissism looks like when it is carried to its logical extreme. These people desire to be worshipped by those they can dominate, as well as the construction of sculptures bearing their likeness, complete obedience, and good reputation. Any disobedience or confrontation is swiftly and violently punished. Perhaps one of the best examples of the intense development of narcissism in the modern era is North Korea. The nation's leaders demanded to be revered as gods and execute and torture anyone who even dared to challenge a notion or idea that didn't align with the dictatorship's ideology.

Why is NLP so infamously contentious? It is covered in Chapter 3.

Right now, you have unrestricted access to the Dark NLP universe. It is important to keep in mind that the principles and methods of this way of thinking directly contradict conventional standards of profound quality, so you should be prepared to have your preconceived notions challenged. This section will begin with several real-world examples of how the power of NLP can positively or negatively impact people's lives. Next, we'll look at some of the most dubious and sinister applications of NLP that have ever been considered. The section will conclude with a look at the range of NLP-based conversations that have taken place over time.

You will get various insights through exploring the discussions that NLP has generated. First of all, you will see that NLP is frequently examined not for its true content but rather for its ability to refute popular belief. Anything that goes against any well-accepted convention will surely spark debate, regardless of what it says. You will also learn about

NLP's ability to provide anyone more influence. Anything that might go against the well-crafted request is seen as dubious, and NLP is no different.

The Effectiveness of NLP: Actual Case Studies

Next, we'll look at various facts on the potential for NLP to change people's lives. This section aims to demonstrate the destructive power of NLP when applied effectively rather than attempting to adopt an ethical stance about the provided NLP models. Every story's ideas will be extracted and made clear so you can understand exactly what happened in each model and why the results happened.

One powerful example of NLP's effectiveness is its ability to help people overcome addictions that hurt their lives. One such tale is a man complaining to an NLP expert about his inability to give up smoking cigarettes. He was spending a significant amount of money on three packs a day and had suffered terrible consequences to his health as a result of his tendency, but he had been unable to find the motivation to give up.

The man's perception of smoking could be replaced by the NLP counsellor using a series of envisioning techniques. The man replaced the connotation of cigarettes with that of death and dreadful well-being rather than viewing them as a luxury. The man had the choice to stop smoking because he was in charge of his inner perception and did not desire to smoke at the moment.

The business world provides yet another example of NLP's power. An innovation organization's high-ranking female executive from its European division was brought to an American meeting with an intimidating CEO. Despite being highly esteemed within her department, she managed to achieve this by being genuinely supportive and friendly to everyone she collaborated with. She was regrettable for the group in America as she lacked a convincing degree of statement.

The woman decided to see an NLP trainer to learn about certain techniques that would help her feel more confident and positive about the meeting in America. She was allowed to link a feeling to a concrete trigger when practising the NLP technique known as secure. She was trained to look back into her history in this particular circumstance to when she felt completely certain and in control of what was happening. This was what she could have done. Then, someone taught her to associate this tendency with a patch of dim light. Then she was instructed to draw a circle around herself on the floor in front of her using this colored light. As a result, the woman experienced an intense sense of total confidence and security within the circle.

The lady may have used this technique to overcome her anxiety about mingling with the leader when it came time for her meeting in America. She could have handled the situation nearby with poise and composure. It turns out that they only wanted to talk to her about strategy and that she wasn't even receiving criticism or punishment. Regardless, she was able to attempt to avoid the negative effects of anxiety and tension because of her NLP preparation.

NLP has been used by some of its most contentious but influential clients in their pursuit of sentiment. In light of NLP's ideas, other methods of thinking are solely focused on displaying enticement; this topic is covered in full later in the book. An overview of how persuasive this can be will be provided, at least until further notice.

The Operation of NLP

You have no control over your circumstances. You do not control life. You cannot govern Nature or other people by acting as God. You are, therefore, the victim of fate.

However, it's up to you how you respond to life. Rather than succumbing to fate, you might accept it as an unexpected and impromptu companion who is excited to accompany you on an exciting journey. Although it might not always be simple, adopting this perspective on life is far better. No matter how hard you try, you can't control life, so why not embrace the curveballs it gives you?

Once more, you will only ever be able to understand reality as you perceive it.

However, altering your perspective on life can be complicated. Grinder and Bandler offer several strategies that can help you achieve it.

Consider life to be an adventure.

Seeing life as an adventure, you can overcome stress and difficulty. Additionally, think of your new NLP strategy as an adventure. In essence, this is an era of inquiry and learning. As you explore your life and your inner thought processes and discover fresh approaches to challenges, you become your own Indiana Jones. Your mind is ready for exploration, like a pristine forest or hidden treasure cave. You are currently investigating numerous aspects of yourself that you do not fully comprehend.

By approaching NLP and life in this way, you're inviting yourself to enjoy yourself. Both the seriousness and the stress are gone. Life and NLP no longer appear like tasks you have to complete; instead, they look like exciting new places to discover and reap abundant benefits. You'll have more excellent drive and enthusiasm for your path to recovery and self-discovery.

Establish Objectives

According to psychological research, the likelihood of accomplishing a goal doubles when one sets one. You feel directionless and aimless when you float through life without any ambitions. Setting goals is crucial while using NLP to change your life and reality. They assist you in determining your goals and, subsequently, in achieving them.

Positive thinking is what NLP prefers to emphasize. Thus, set constructive goals. Consider gains rather than negative thoughts like "I want to stop being so negative" or "I want to lose eighteen pounds." "I want to get more fit and toned muscles," or "I want to get happier." The gain will motivate you to work toward success since it has more beneficial effects than loss. Gaining something is often far more accessible for the mind to process than losing something.

Consider what your true desires are. Don't base your ambitions on what you believe you should want or what others think you should desire. Instead, build your goals on what you want in life. For example, someone might advise purchasing a house when you're thirty. However, you most likely detest the thought of shelling out a ton of cash to own a house. Instead, you are concerned with making a house uniquely yours; the money is only one aspect. Consider living in a home instead of purchasing one if it is what you value more. Naturally, this implies that you will eventually own property, but make sure your objectives are centred around what truly matters to you.

State your objectives in terms of your genuine aspirations. You'll then be more driven to accomplish them.

Making objectives emotionally fulfilling is beneficial. Your emotions greatly influence your thoughts. You are more likely to put in the mental effort to accomplish a goal if you have an emotional connection to it.

The Levels of Neurology

At the most basic level of the environment, humans respond to the world around us and influence it and the people living there. This is our experience's "where" and "when."

Our behaviours are the things we do. They comprise the ideas we compute and can be purposeful or reflexive. The "what" of our experience is this.

Our ability constrains our actions. We can't learn anything about a person's ability from their inaction. However, when they do, their actions suggest ability. Our knowledge, skills, and tactics make up our capabilities. This is our experience's "how."

Values and beliefs are sometimes stated in isolation and other times in conjunction. I would rather keep them apart.

What we consider to be accurate are our beliefs. They both restrict our options and grant us a license to act.

Values are the things we believe to be significant. As such, they control our decisions and inspire us.

Our values and beliefs may coincide or run counter to one another. However, taken as a whole, they determine how much we can develop and use skills. They serve as our experience's "why."

Your identity is the fundamental sense of who you are. This always crosses over with values or the things you believe are significant in your life. Your identity will determine your life's principles, sense of direction, and perceived mission. The "kind of person" you think you are is shaped by your identity. This represents our experience of "who am I."

The spiritual level, or your sense of purpose, is the deepest. It links you to something greater than yourself and transcends your sense of self. This could be a spiritual connection, neighbourhood, organization, or larger society. It provides significance to your life and decisions and is the foundation for what you believe and do. This is our experience's "who or what else."

How NLP Uses Neurological Levels

This concept is primarily applied in change work, where it assists individuals in making personal changes.

First, we can identify conflicts impeding more productive behaviours and, consequently, better results using replies at various logical levels. This is at the values level, for instance, if I enjoy hanging out with my friends and they are essential to me. However, my ambition to advance my talents may clash with my boss's request that I accept a secondment to a foreign city to do so.

After that, we can assist someone in bringing their many levels of interpretation of a circumstance into alignment. We can help them understand what is best for them and instil new zeal in them to seek it by bringing them into harmony.

People can make significant decisions more effectively by working through logical levels, especially if they're stuck or need clarification on what they want.

The Idea of NLP

Neuro-linguistic programming is referred to as NLP. Neuro refers to a nervous system connection. The language we use is referred to as linguistic. Neuro-linguistics studies the language your body speaks to your neural system. In this instance, a program is something that activates your neurological system by stimulating your brain's feedback system. It describes the thoughts and products that come from your brain.

Leading names in this field are Drs. John Grinder and Richard Bandler. They made NLP more accessible so that even the average person could comprehend and learn its essential ideas. Since we have profited from these two experts for a considerable time, society owes them and should remember them.

After the 18th century, psychology became more popular, and more people are now researching human behaviour in general and the development of the human brain in particular, among many other related topics. More than ever before, researchers have worked to understand humans' origins, habits, and beliefs. They researched a wide range of issues, including anxiety, depression, and repression, all of which were first studied by academics around 1950. Drs.Bandler and Grinder conducted research between 1950 and 1970 that demonstrated innovative approaches to working with human psychology. They designed these studies rapidly to make NLP useful to everyone researching mind programming for better living. Although many people can benefit from the NLP programs at lesser levels of training, the programs' creators intended for readers to assist them in reaching master-level training.

The NLP idea is centred on your thoughts and feelings during emotional reactions, not a psychological diagnosis. NLP is made up of the mental and bodily responses that take place in the following scenarios:

1. When you are experiencing anger 2. When you are at ease

3. Whenever you use tobacco

4. When you have a lot of energy

5. When you're not feeling well

6. When you're experiencing depression

With the help of neuro-linguistic programming, you can modify your thoughts, perspective on the past, outlook on life, and physical and mental responses. Additionally, it teaches you to take charge of your body and mind, which leads to a better and more fruitful existence.

The distinction between NLP and hypnosis

Hypnosis is another scientific technique for managing emotions. Our brain's four-wave phases are alpha, beta, delta, and theta.

Delta waves create a better, transcendental condition. A person in beta provides the typical waking state. Theta waves are between alpha and delta waves. The brain is affected by alpha waves up to 200 times more than by beta waves, and when you meditate, many amazing ideas surface. To help patients better train their thoughts, alpha waves are researched during meditation and sleep at several training facilities. These centres produce a type of "brain dream."

On the spectrum, theta waves are situated between delta and alpha waves. The number of cycles per second varies depending on the type of wave: delta waves happen 3-6 times per second, theta waves 7-10 times per second, alpha waves 11-16 times per second, and beta waves 16-20 times per second. Being in an alpha cycle continuously will improve your ability to focus.

One can tell what state individuals are in. People who drive, for instance, are frequently in the alpha state. Even after we arrive home, there are moments when we feel as though we did not complete the entire journey. Similarly, time seems to pass quickly when we watch television; three hours of content happen quickly.

Kids who play video games also make this clear. They frequently don't get sidetracked from the game for very long. This is usually the state individuals are in when playing video games. You can see that they are all everyday actions, which is why this study was conducted. The six key steps of hypnotherapy are pre-talk, induction, deepening, script, amnesia, and termination. Every action has a distinct goal in mind to achieve positive programming. However, NLP does not employ these same procedures and methods. In a hypnotherapy session, the patient is largely still while the therapist speaks; in a neurolinguistic programming (NLP) session, the patient actively participates in a few exercises to rewire their brain while awake. Both the NLP system and hypnosis have benefits.

After completing your NLP Practitioner certificate course, I suggest moving on to the next phase and earning your Master Practitioner and Train the Trainer certifications. You will gain a deeper comprehension of NLP as a result.

If you have more time, I also suggest attending therapy sessions for two or three hours a week, which can help you with a variety of concerns like getting rid of negative ideas, conquering phobias, and managing family problems, overexcitement, sadness, or anxiety. Therapy can also assist you in accessing your subconscious mind to process challenging emotions to improve your life. NLP and hypnosis are two distinct approaches to therapy. I recommend that you find a mentor to help you learn these methods.

Chapter 4: Essential Rules for Reading and Evaluating Individuals

In this chapter, we'll go over some broad principles that you may apply to people analysis and reading. Please remember that you are subject to these rules as well. So do remember them, as being aware of them will assist you in avoiding giving contradictory messages.

Having a list of principles, axioms, and guidelines handy when debating the subject of people analysis will help you better understand the thoughts and emotions that support the conscious message that those around you are conveying.

Therefore, even though they are not infallible, these guidelines provide useful guidance on turning your knowledge of human nature into something practical and beneficial when interacting with others in social or professional contexts.

Therefore, these guidelines are generally applicable. They do have universal application worldwide and apply to all cultures. Therefore, you may be confident that you will receive knowledge that will give you the upper hand in your interpersonal connections.

Remember that your comprehension of these guidelines will also grow as time goes on. As a result, you will become more insightful the more you engage with others and witness these guidelines in action. In the future, you will be able to depend on this.

The first general rule of thumb to consider is how individuals speak. This could get confusing if you are conversing with someone whose first language is not English. As a result, their native tongue may significantly influence their pronunciation, tone, intonation, and pitch. Nonetheless, you will notice recurring themes in people's speaking patterns.

For example, when someone is anxious or disturbed, they usually speak more quickly. Although this is nothing new, it should be mentioned that when people are anxious or upset, they will involuntarily return to their original accent. This is evident when people are distressed or under duress. Under intense emotion, their natural accent will emerge because their instincts precede their conscious thought.

Pitch is an additional example of speech patterns. When people become upset, their naturally high-pitched voices become even higher. Conversely, those with a lower voice tone will abruptly switch to a higher tone. Given that a higher vocal tone indicates distress, this response is very understandable. Therefore, hearing someone speaking louder than usual could be their response to a stressful circumstance.

One last thing regarding inflexions. People will usually slow down when they want to make an argument. People naturally respond this way to ensure their opponent has grasped what they are saying. This is a regular occurrence for lecturers and professors. Pausing or slowing down tells the audience it is time to focus.

Laughing and smiling are two more general guidelines to remember.

Now, people will smile and even laugh out of the blue when they are truly happy and enjoying themselves. Children are an excellent indicator of this. Youngsters who are content and enjoying themselves constantly chuckle. As it happens, having a room full of rowdy children is a positive thing. It indicates that they are at ease and secure. Youngsters will abruptly become silent if they sense any kind of threat or fear.

People always respond in this way throughout their lives. But as people get older, things do tend to change a bit. For example, you could notice that certain people tend to laugh nervously or smile excessively, particularly in awkward situations.

The explanation is that people try to be friendly to someone who might want to harm them. In the wild, animals will naturally assume a defensive and aggressive posture, whereas people will try to be friendly toward anyone who might try to harm them. Of all, uneasy laughter does precious little to prevent someone from harming you if that is their intention.

Some people in the corporate sector may go out of control during meetings and get-togethers. In reality, most people are just trying to make others like them; they are just trying to grab attention by their antics, which is why most people ignore them.

The class clown is another illustration of this. Someone who has been branded as the class clown desperately attempts to fit in. Therefore, all of their jokes, laughing, and outwardly upbeat demeanour are just attempts to win over others.

Compared to someone who is the life of the party, someone who displays a gloomy and even unpleasant disposition may be acting considerably more truthfully. Of course, treating others rudely has no justification. However, the fundamental idea is that someone always attempting to be clever and humorous is merely attempting to blend in and win their peers' approval.

Neuro-Linguistic Programming: What Is It?

Is it possible to change how your brain functions by recording how it reacts to stimuli and utilizing language and other forms of communication to impact its behaviour? That's what NLP is, after all. It was created and popularised by a linguist and therapist named Dr. Richard Bandler in the 1970s. It mostly entails combining self-hypnosis and hypnosis with hypnosis to create the necessary results.

What is the process of NLP?

NLP may be applied to any facet of interpersonal and personal relationships since it possesses contemporary psychology's most advantageous, practical, and approachable aspects. Consider it. Have you ever tried to break a bad habit but ultimately found yourself going back to it? Did you take a moment to consider why you adopted your previous habits again?

Your elders' responses to certain danger factors taught you how to respond to them as a child. These reactions can include a phobia of snakes or spiders. Your parents or other elders taught you to dread snakes by fleeing from them. Since that fear was stored in the subconscious, it can only be released by accessing that part of the mind. Negative emotions and limiting behaviours outweigh your optimistic conscious thoughts. The unconscious mind stores the habits you develop throughout your life; therefore, you must access the unconscious mind to break them.

NLP essentially functions by enabling you to see and comprehend the changes in your life, both good and bad, and to modify the ones that don't feel right for you.

Motivation, goal-setting, overcoming addictions and bad habits, developing a positive self-image and self-esteem, public speaking, managing allergies and asthma, depression, phobias and fears, eating disorders and weight control, business coaching, mental and physical healing, and confidence-boosting are all areas where NLP can be used.

Using NLP can help you become more self-aware and recognize and respect the emotions and behavioural patterns of others, which can lead to improved cooperation and empathy. It also aids in improving your communication abilities for any kind of sales and customer service.

The second idea is sensory consciousness.

Everybody occasionally experiences highs and lows in their senses. When your senses focus primarily on what is happening around you rather than within you, you are in high external awareness. In the former, your primary focus is on your ideas and feelings on the inside.

Qualitatively, each state is equally important, but not in certain situations. Consider it. Do you sometimes struggle to come up with a thoughtful answer when someone asks you an unprepared question? How would you feel, for example, about seeing your former partner again? This could be useful in this situation. Going too low, however, during a speech in front of an audience can result in increased nervousness, inefficiency, or a disconnection from the audience, all of which are neither helpful nor required. Every day, when conversing, you tend to get carried away and focus too much on responding instead of paying attention and observing. You could miss many things the person in question is going through due to this prolonged period of low time when you are speaking with them, making your communication highly ineffective.

When you find the result of your desire, you need to be sufficiently aware of your senses to judge whether you are headed in the right direction. Repetition of someone else's words does not necessarily indicate that you are listening. NLP is useful in this situation. NLP assists you in focusing on enhanced awareness of those around you in certain ways, including the capacity to recognize and decipher variations in voice, muscle tone, linguistic patterns, skin tone, eye movements, and respiration rate. Just consider. When I asked you how you felt about seeing your ex again, did you notice that you seemed to be seeing something in your mind? NLP uses these and other indicators to determine the effect you can have on others; in other words, it's just feedback on how you responded.

Take a Mental Tour

After learning all 13 of the best communication techniques, I have a few additional suggestions for you to work on to assist you in reaching your goals and improving how strong and successful the 13 tips are when used. But before we move forward, you must comprehend your thoughts. Have you ever considered the inner workings of your mind? How does one begin and conclude the process of thinking?

When used well, your mind is an extremely strong tool that can perform amazing feats for you.

I hope to clarify what "conscious mind" and "subconscious mind" mean in this chapter. Although everyone uses these two terms rather frequently, nobody truly understands them. First, let's define the terms conscious and subconscious minds clearly.

Your mind typically functions on three levels: the conscious, the subconscious, and the unconscious. For now, we will only be discussing the conscious and subconscious minds. The rational level is also called your conscious mind, and the irrational level is your subconscious. It is crucial to comprehend how these two parts of your mind function because they operate in various ways.

Your conscious mind is the part of your mind that you have total control over. You are well aware that your ideas might be described as "good," "bad," "happy," "sad," and so forth. It is possible for you to deliberately introduce either positive or negative ideas into your head. Your subconscious mind, which often handles mental processes behind the scenes, is indirectly influenced by the thoughts you are fully aware of thinking. Your subconscious mind programs your thoughts and turns them into your ingrained habits. Whatever you think percolates into your subconscious mind. Your habitual thought patterns cause you to respond in the manner that your subconscious mind has preprogrammed. Your subconscious mind would never challenge your waking awareness regarding right and wrong. It just stores the data entered into the system and responds to your actions in that specific manner.

Let me clarify this using a straightforward example from your day-to-day existence. Typically, you wash your hands after finishing your meal.

You don't consciously tell your mind to go wash your hands. Is it not?

Please remember when you were requested to wash your hands after eating for the first time. After every meal, you had begun deliberately training your mind to wash your hands. That concept of yours had left an imprint and registered in your subconscious. After repeatedly performing the same action, it developed into a habit, and you now wash your hands right after every meal.

You must also be aware of another crucial aspect of your conscious and subconscious minds. Our subconscious mind can't comprehend words like "no," "don't," "not," and "never." You must learn to reword these words so that your subconscious mind sees what you truly want because your subconscious mind cannot comprehend or register these words.

Allow me to use you as an example to demonstrate what I mean when we say our subconscious mind does not understand those words. Follow my instructions below to the letter.

Advice: Avoid picturing a black cat.

What instantly sprang to mind?

A negro cat! Is it not?

Did you know that the word "not" is incomprehensible to your subconscious mind? Therefore, we need to exercise extreme caution in what we believe and subconsciously commit to memory.

Step 1: Comprehending What Mindfulness Is

The first thing you need to do is figure out what mindfulness is. Techniques like mindfulness have been around since the beginning of time. It is designed to assist individuals in staying in the present and preventing stray thoughts and feelings. As was previously noted, busy lives are becoming the norm, and many people need a way to let off steam. Being mindful can be that vent.

The emphasis of mindfulness is on maintaining single-task focus at all times. Thus, you need to focus on the current task rather than thinking about other things. You undoubtedly recall your instructor telling you to focus on your notes in class and avoid getting sidetracked by anything around you. The idea of awareness is the same. You have to block out the outside world and concentrate on whatever you are doing.

It's easier said than done, of course. Most people are accustomed to getting sidetracked by objects and happenings around them. We have trouble focusing on one subject; instead, we frequently glance about or let our thoughts go to unrelated activities. That is precisely the thing that makes us feel more stressed. We put off doing our assignment and kept extending the deadline. Then we get stressed out and fret about the unfinished work. Furthermore, we become more tense and anxious due to our worries about the diversions.

But awareness will stop all of that. We shall learn to prioritize our work and pay attention to nothing else. It will instruct us to let go of the past and find contentment in the present. Turning off distractions and increasing focus is the essence of mindfulness.

Why Visualization Is Effective—As Is All Of Nlp.

Now, you might be wondering what the fundamental ideas are underlying NLP visualization. We'll deconstruct NLP into its component parts so you can better grasp the approach.

"N" is a prefix for "neuro," the word for the brain. Neurons are specialized cells that make up your brain. These are the sense cells in your body. Your brain's neurons all have distinct functions, yet they must cooperate for the brain to function as a whole. Despite their striking resemblance, your frontal lobes and cerebellum cells perform fundamentally different jobs.

Your brain forms its neural networks through specific brain functions. After that, they adjust to the new perspectives. Learning new abilities creates new neural connections in the brain. NLP is a technique to change your brain circuits and generate new behaviours.

The "linguistic," or "L" in NLP, means language. Everybody has a private inner monologue. This is the voice that only you hear. This might change during the day and be either positive or negative. We use this voice to remind ourselves of the purpose of entering a space or plan our next action.

We employ this voice to determine our behaviour and self-perception. Are you more likely to compliment or criticize yourself? Do you have a bad attitude? The goal of NLP is to modify your internal dialogue so that you can become more optimistic, create objectives, and ultimately modify your behaviour.

The letter "P" represents programming. Computer science is another term for programming. The human brain, however, functions as a biological computer. This indicates that the brain's internal language is its software, and its neurons are its hardware. The computer can be programmed to produce an output by combining these two. You can better grasp NLP by using this analogy. You can get the desired function with the appropriate hardware and software. What NLP can do for you is this.

An essential component of neuro-linguistic programming is visualization. The basic idea behind visualization is that you may picture yourself getting somewhere you wish to go. Visualization is a simple process that has significant outcomes. You can picture a goal, a solution, or a technique to tackle an issue just by shutting your eyes.

Through visualization, you might picture yourself carrying out a task you have never done before or devise a novel method to complete it. This enables you to talk to yourself using fresh vocabulary and in a different context. You will begin to exhibit new behaviours after these neural connections are established and you come to terms with the new language. Someone has modified your brain.

Visualization relies heavily on your capacity to see things as you would. We call this dissociation and association. As we saw in the last example, you imagined doing things your way (association) and your colleague doing them (dissociation) when you had to take over a presentation for an injured colleague's work. This can be seen as an audience member or role-playing situation on stage.

Let's look into modelling when you have learned the fundamentals of NLP. We covered modelling in Chapter 1 as a means of fictitiously substituting a wounded colleague at a crucial business meeting. Let's investigate more closely.

Fundamental Modeling for Mental Health

Modelling is not the same as showcasing new goods or styles in neuro-linguistic programs. Modelling is watching and rewiring the brain to achieve what another person or method has achieved. Even though every person is different and has a unique story, modelling can help you identify your current situation and desired future direction. Though they might not know it, kids frequently emulate their parents' behaviours. Because toddlers frequently imitate their parents and other caregivers, adults must watch how they act around kids. Older kids will mimic their favourite basketball player's batting motion or even shoot free throws similarly. Kids can learn to sing like famous musicians or memorize passages from their favourite movies. Almost everyone has engaged in what is known as external modelling at some point in their lives.

A more inward kind of modelling is NLP. It enables you to alter your behaviour, accomplish your goals, and succeed in everything you do. You probably know some persons in the acting or writing professions you admire. Perhaps you both share a similar background or region or perhaps find their work or performance inspiring. You could have read articles or biographies about this individual. Celebrities' everyday life can now be followed on social media platforms like Twitter and Instagram.

You likely know more about an influential person in your desired work sector. Here's when modelling becomes useful. Consider the reasons for this person's achievement and how those factors contributed to it. You can leverage your visualization techniques by modelling your thoughts and mental language after successful people. This will assist you in moulding your actions to align with their achievements. If you want to be an action movie star, you won't become Jason Statham overnight. You can use the acting styles of your favourite performers to help you visualize your achievement.

This is an advanced modelling objective. In the future, we will investigate extensive modelling methodologies. Let's start our modelling activities by discussing a basic concept. Now, let's return to our fictitious colleague. It is now your chance to deliver John's important business presentation once you have recovered from the shock of his injuries.

What action do you take first? You will have to obtain his presentation materials in person. It's as easy as finding his charts and graphs in his office. Any digital files you save on a shared drive at work may also exist. It's critical to mentally prepare yourself to deliver the presentation with the same expertise and accuracy as John. Here's when modelling becomes useful.

Examine the reasons behind John's hiring. Was it his experience, manner, or seniority that made the difference? All three, combined with other variables, most likely make up the solution. Considering John's effectiveness and communication style in these meetings is important. Do they seem amiable and personable? Or are they formal and businesslike? Can he respond to inquiries from customers in a kind manner?

After you have addressed every question, it is your turn to model. For a brief moment, close your eyes and visualize John delivering the lecture. Observe his attitude and mannerisms. After you have a clear image, put yourself in John's position. Envision yourself delivering the talk and responding to any inquiries. Imagine concluding the transaction by shaking hands with your clients.

This representation will aid your presentation planning. To succeed as much as you would have had John been present, you may take on his persona and emulate his actions. Greetings on your fictitious transaction!

Observing those around you as a model for daily living can be beneficial. Follow your well-organized friend's lead to enhance your organizational abilities. Take a seat with your sister and watch her prepare food. You can improve as a cook by taking tips from your sister.

By using it consistently, modelling can be applied to mind management. Modelling and visualization help you create new neural pathways all the time. As new neural connections are formed, you will notice a shift in your behaviour and self-talk. Modelling and visualization will be the foundation for every other NLP application in this book.

How Are NLP and Dark Psychology Related to One Another?

For many people who are not psychologists, neuro-linguistic programming, or NLP, has become a popular way to discuss human thought and communication. A variation of popular psychology is used. You need to be aware of some communication and nonverbal tactics, even though criticizing NLP is well outside the purview of our talk (since it would address multiple concerns). That's meant to be effective, and purported master practitioners and respectable and dubious instructors are pushing it. In contrast to popular or mainstream fields like psychology, neurology, or linguistics, which are grounded in controlled studies and academic research, NLP is more concerned with "what works" and draws many of its techniques from other fields that are used in real-world settings. Thus, even if there may be substantial research backing for several non-verbal communication NLP approaches and assertions, it's also possible that some methods and arguments haven't been properly validated in controlled study settings.

For students who are not serious about nonverbal communication, reading about NLP can expose you to fantastic and correct ideas from disciplines like linguistics and psychology. However, it will also introduce you to theories and presumptions that have not been proven true or may not be true. The issue is that depending on NLP courses and material won't allow you to determine what is and isn't valid. NLP is more of a patchwork of helpful concepts than a cohesive philosophy.

To make matters worse, NLP has drawn untrained or unscrupulous individuals because it mostly relies on advertisements and arguments, in contrast to more scientific, science-based disciplines. And who, with due respect, may be referred to as New Age practitioners?

To elucidate the variety of items that certain practitioners incorporate into

NLP, let me say that the concept or principles are taken from linguistics, which is undoubtedly a legitimate and accepted perspective on communication. The hypnotic regression of former lives, well outside the bounds of recognized scientific practice, is at the other extreme. Both are considered a component of NLP. Then, to be clear, you may find specialists and marketing claims that teach you how to use NLP techniques to captivate women and detect lies in individuals by observing their eye movements.

This is meant to explain why more conventional, thoroughly studied, and controlled domains do not have non-verbal behavioural characteristics specifically drawn from NLP. Many of the topics covered in this topic ARE related to NLP, but they are included because they were created before or independently of the NLP community.

The idea underlying NLP is that skilled communicators build relationships with others by utilizing common verbal and nonverbal communication strategies. Such methods are predicated on an awareness of the internal sensory interpretation frameworks humans employ to make sense of and interpret their experiences. A comprehensive NLP training program aims to give you a highly developed understanding of identifying and reacting to this extremely delicate communication. This is because a large portion of the "magic" of NLP is dependent on this one of the essential talents. To use most of the well-known NLP procedures, create outstanding relationships, train someone in personal development, or speak professionally, you must possess the rare capacity to perceive non-verbal communication.

To help you convey the objectives and aspirations of the unconscious mind to the conscious self, NLP is similar to a user manual for the brain. Suppose you are travelling to a distant nation and want chicken wings. You go to a restaurant and order the same, but the food arrives with liver stew due to a misunderstanding.

Because so much of what is unconscious is lost in translation regarding the conscious self, humans frequently fail to identify and acknowledge these unconscious thoughts and desires.

The concept is that your unconscious mind wants you to have whatever you truly want, but you will never pursue your desires if your conscious mind ignores the message.

NLP was created with the help of successful role models who were also exceptional therapists and communicators.

The study of NLP focuses on how the human mind combines perception, ideas, and behaviours to satisfy its basic needs. Our mind uses sophisticated neural networks to analyze information, give it meaning through verbal or auditory cues, and store these signals in patterns to create and retain new memories.

We can consciously employ and apply specific tools and approaches to change our ideas and behaviours to accomplish our goals. These methods we can employ to manage our and other people's minds are perceptual, behavioural, and conversational.

One of the main tenets of NLP is that the "Preferred Representational System (PRS)" is the sensory system that our conscious mind is predisposed to. Expressions such as "I hear you" or "Sounds good" indicate a PRS that is auditory, whereas "I see you" may indicate a visual PRS.

A licensed therapist can determine patients' PRS and tailor their therapy approach accordingly. Among other things, this therapeutic framework frequently entails goal-setting, information collection, and rapport-building.

More people are utilizing NLP to support self-improvement, including confidence building and self-reflection, as well as developing social skills, chiefly communication.

NLP training and therapy can be provided through language- and sensory-based therapies, utilizing behaviour modification strategies tailored to each client's needs to enhance social communication and boost self-esteem and self-awareness.

NLP trainers and therapists work to help their clients realize that their perspective of the world and how they behave in it are closely related and that the first step to a brighter future is gaining a deep awareness of who they are and making contact with their unconscious mind.

Why People Who Manipulate Do So

Now that you can recognize subtle and emotional manipulation techniques with some proficiency, let's examine the motivations behind the manipulation. This could make handling them easier for you.

Every one of us has experienced terrible smear campaigns, pathological lying, and being made to feel inadequate. They defy all rational expectations of human conduct. What causes someone to become an evil manipulator? Why do manipulators employ certain strategies? What drives them to use deceitful tactics to get their way with people and disregard social norms?

dread

What motivates someone to use deception to further their own goals? Easy peasy - fear!

Manipulators are concerned that they will never be able to use their skills to achieve the desired result. People and life will not favourably treat them if they behave morally. They function under the premise that individuals are life and that people are set up to oppose them. People who manipulate others see everyone as their enemy and think things won't always work out for them, even if they behave well.

There's a concern that things are scarce and that others will benefit if they don't.

They believe individuals must be subdued to achieve their goals since it is a dog-eat-dog world. This control can take any shape, including practical, psychological, emotional, and financial. They seek to exert control over others to accomplish their goals and allay their fears.

Manipulators experience dread and insecurity all the time. "What if it doesn't work out?" "How will I feel if my partner moves on to someone else?" "What if I lose the upper hand to someone else?" To combat an innate sense of anxiety, they constantly seek to dominate and win.

Where is the source of this fear? It stems from a profound feeling of unworthiness. This means, "I do not deserve the good things and people in life; therefore, they will depart from me." I have to use some cunning strategies that will give me complete control over the people and things I don't deserve to keep them from leaving me. The fundamental idea is, to put it briefly, "I am undeserving or unworthy of people and things!"

Poor or Absent Consciousness
Conscience deficiency is one other underlying cause of manipulation. People are more likely to act without conscience when they don't recognize responsibility for their reality. A fair system does not exist in the minds of

manipulators. They have also ceased to evolve. They don't strive for unity between their inner feelings and the outside world or attempt to draw lessons from past mistakes.

Even when these outcomes haven't satisfied them, they see manipulation as a safe and secure way to achieve the desired outcome. They never learn their lesson; emotionally and psychologically, they keep returning to where they were before. They will come up with another excuse to manipulate to evade this lesson. As a result, individuals become mired in a vicious cycle of unworthiness or discontent, which feeds the demand for further manipulation.

Since the manipulative behaviour is not genuine, equitable, or successful, it is ineffective after the initial temporary repair. It is a protective mechanism in response to hurt, unworthiness, fear, or insecurity. The manipulator is trying to counteract these feelings by becoming manipulative.

Manipulation is a purposeful action that is not in line with one's conscience or the greater good. The individual doesn't function under the tenet that "we are one," which implies that authenticity is preferred over non-authenticity while attempting to manipulate others. Anything obtained by deception simply results in small wins, continuous difficulties, emptiness or fear, and unworthiness. This produces an even greater sense of unworthiness. Unworthiness, once more, is the dread that one is undeserving of the love and approval of others.

Manipulative people never grow or learn the value of being true to themselves. Knowing that one is loved and accepted for who one truly is prevents one from realizing the true power of honesty and merit. Fundamentally, the root of manipulation is frequently a sense of unworthiness.

They refuse to pay the price necessary to achieve their objectives.

Individuals who do not want to pay the price necessary to achieve their goals frequently employ manipulation to further their interests. They frequently work hard to achieve the goal or fulfil their purpose without wishing to reciprocate or bear the cost.

For example, the relationship will require work if you want your partner to stay with you. In addition to much more, you'll need to provide your partner with love, empathy, comprehension, patience, loyalty, inspiration, support, and a stable future.

Although a manipulator may not want their spouse to leave them, they also do not want to bear the costs associated with keeping their lover in a stable, happy, and healthy relationship where they will never have to say goodbye.

They want their spouse to stick around even if they may not want to be faithful or spend much time with them. People unwilling to pay the price to get what they want may turn to deceitful or manipulative means of achieving their objectives without bearing the consequences.

Similarly, a manipulative person will use deception to gain a position in their organization rather than exerting effort, staying late, learning new skills, or obtaining a degree. The individual is unwilling to invest the necessary time or money to advance.

In some situations, someone has a strong psychological belief that having wishes is wrong or that having any desires will make them appear arrogant. Then, using manipulation to get what they want or need without even asking for it becomes a tactic.

Manipulators are aware that everything has a cost. Nobody will do them a favour if they don't anticipate receiving something in return. If they don't act with thanks and kindness, they won't be able to keep acquiring stuff. They need to show commitment, loyalty, and love in return for someone to love them and have sex with them. By attempting to obtain something without paying the associated cost, manipulators attempt to push their luck. It's usually the simplest solution.

Chapter 1: Dark Psychology And Manipulation

Dark Psychology: What Is It?

Dark psychology is the practice of mind control and manipulation. The dark triad, also known as the Dark triad, is a psychological profile that is determined by combining the subsequent elements:

An example of psychopathy is: This is a characteristic of a person or people who have a hard exterior, are "callous," act cruelly, and have very little empathy. These people are apathetic, frequently cynical and insensitive and lack empathy, regret, morality, and ethical standards.

Machiavellianism: This group comprises those who are exceedingly manipulative and have an air of superficial charm. For example, some people can lie, take advantage of others they can cheat on, and cheat to acquire what they desire.

Beliefs of superiority, grandiosity, vanity, and strong emotional explosiveness are characteristics of narcissism. These individuals believe they should have a higher social position and expect special treatment; if they are not given the treatment they deserve, they may become angry, irrational, or violent. They want everyone to respect and notice them.

Additionally, they are typically aggressive, irresponsible, and dishonest individuals who treat others poorly (even though they may appear charming on the outside). They also have little self-control and can act extremely kind one moment before losing it.

There is a significant gender disparity because, in contrast to other personality profiles (such as an anxious profile), this personality profile is far more common in males than in women.

What Constitutes A Manipulative Action?

The core of manipulative behaviour is deception. Very manipulative people are skilled at deceit, and combined with their (common) coldness, they are vicious.

Those who frequently manipulate others do not view others as sentient beings but as tools to accomplish a task.

This frequently implies that they won't hesitate to abandon you by the side of the road once they have reached their "destination."

The worst aspect is that they occasionally try to make you look guilty while making themselves appear the victim. That's the challenging issue with manipulative individuals. Small things like making you come to their office or surprising you are only a couple of their traits, among many others. This is consistent with intimidation, another crucial component of manipulative behaviours.

Because it maintains their position of authority and elevates them above others, manipulators like intimidating and demeaning people.

People manipulate for the sake of status, money, power, or vanity. Thus, manipulation frequently results in one's circumstances improving (at the expense of others!)

Reasons Behind Manipulative Actions

Regrettably, it is accurate to say that those who exhibit manipulative tendencies in their early years have either experienced trauma or mistreatment.

For example, a child who experiences physical or mental abuse from narcissistic parents may end up expressing himself in very negative ways.

People may act manipulatively when there is a lot on the line, as in politics.

Once they have experienced it, a certain class of people will stop at nothing to maintain their position of power, no matter the cost.

Politicians and managers are among the many selfish individuals who will stop at nothing to hold onto their position of authority.

This also explains why a "ladder" of individuals who will stop at nothing to remain "at the top" is established in schools and colleges.

The parties, fancy homes and vehicles, pricey timepieces, and high-end apparel revolve around them to project an air of power. These folks frequently exhibit narcissism as well.

On the other hand, certain people are inherently prone to manipulative behaviour, and these individuals are frequently observed in several of the previously listed scenarios. Another term for these individuals is psychopaths.

Methods Employed in the Field of Dark Psychology

How Can One Apply Dark Psychology?

Dark psychology encompasses a vast array of mental strategies. Thus, it's critical to realize that each has a unique application. Even though some approaches overlap, it can be useful to define each to fully understand the range of dark psychology.

Convincing

Convincing someone to act or think a specific way through argumentation or logic is persuasion. In dark psychology, persuasion refers to persuading someone to do something that will benefit the persuader but may not benefit the subject. Coercion or other forms of forced obedience may be used to achieve this.

In business, persuasion is crucial for sales, but it may also be applied in interpersonal interactions. Individuals who are being persuaded are typically conscious of what is happening yet helpless to stop it. Since the time of the Ancient Greeks, when Aristotle taught his students rhetoric and argumentation techniques, persuasion has been taught as a separate academic field.

Picture Source: Persuasion in Action

Trickery

Even without the negative connotations associated with dark psychology, manipulation is associated with undesirable outcomes. Manipulation is the ability to shape something to fit your needs and preferences, to bend something to your will, or to move its parts until they fit together perfectly. This is a term used in dark psychology to describe the process of getting someone to act on behalf of the one influencing them, alter who they are, or behave in a way that is inconsistent with who they are.

Because competent manipulators can easily put their subjects at ease, those frequently influenced aren't even aware that it's happening. Even when there are telltale signs, they are typically promptly disregarded or overlooked as the manipulation progresses. While psychologists are still attempting to determine the precise trigger for manipulation, some have determined what they consider to be the most salient traits of both the manipulator and the manipulated.

Mental well-being

The history of NLP shows that it started as a psychology or mental health method. As noted in Mastering the NLP Communication Model, a psychiatrist and other therapists were among the early influences. As such, its methods give the duly certified practitioner access to a vast array of easy-to-use yet powerful instruments. Treatments for addictions, tension, anxiety, and phobias can all be effectively handled with it.

The NLP Communication Model can be used to explain why this is feasible. Anxiety and stress, or phobias and fears, are at the core of most mental illnesses. These circumstances are states, and internal representations and filters are intimately associated with these states. As such, they offer the best chances for the certified NLP Practitioner.

Please take note that I am mentioning the need for qualification because if a certified practitioner or someone with some NLP skills starts treating mental disorders without the proper approval from the relevant mental health authorities, there may be consequences, including fines or jail time. It is true that Tony Robbins, who began by performing phobia cures in public, was acting illegally. This does not imply, however, that he was not successful. However, I advise exercising caution and abiding by the law.

I started by sharing with you the VK-Dissociation technique, commonly used to heal phobias, in The Basis of NLP Techniques. This is an incredibly effective, quick double dissociation intervention. It controls the state typically elicited by recalling the initial event by altering the meta-programs and internal representations. The steps are as follows:

1) Ascertain security. I prefer to imply that the subject will instantly feel safe and secure if I speak a certain word or touch them on the shoulder or wrist. I might first ask them to picture a location where they feel safe, and then I might speak or touch them to help them correlate that image with safety. I watch for any indications that they might start to painfully revindicate during the method, and I'm ready to pull the safety anchor if necessary.

2) I urge them to picture themselves preparing to watch a movie while seated in a cosy and secure theatre.

3) I urge them to picture themselves as viewers of themselves while seated in

the projectionist booth. This separation is thus doubled.

4) I advise them to begin watching a movie of the first sensitizing incident if I think it is acceptable. They think that this is the incident that started the phobia. Once more, I'm looking closely for any indications that I should activate their safety anchor.

5) I recommend they experiment with the submodalities as soon as they start watching the film. A few instances include turning the sound down, muting it, playing the video in reverse, turning it black and white or grainy, etc. This is the stage where their internal representation gets deprogrammed.

6) After helping them visualize themselves as audience members, I will repeat the deprogramming step once I believe they have finished it. It is a single dissociation at this stage.

7) If I see no red flags and believe that the deprogramming and dissociations have been effective, I can urge them to close their eyes, continue to calm their thoughts, and end the state by telling them that they will be back in the present moment when they open their eyes.

Numerous more effective NLP interventions exist to deprogram problematic thinking patterns, including parts integration, reframing, collapsing negative anchors, and a range of temporal regression approaches.

Chapter 1: Comprehend Deception

A manipulation is a form of social influence where the objectives are to use direct or indirect strategies to change the behaviour or perception of others.

Since the manipulator's goals are frequently advanced at the expense of another, such tactics may be seen as cunning and exploitative.

The idea of exercise is not always detrimental to social influence, even though social influence or impact may indicate deceptive manipulation depending on the situation and reasons.

Make the most of your basic tools. Be kind but tough, make the most of your time, avoid accepting responsibility for your actions, and ask probing questions.

One effective tactic to divert attention from you and back toward your manipulator is asking questions. They may find this annoying since, particularly if they have been controlling you previously, they don't anticipate you to inquire. It works well to startle them and help them realize how to play the game. Be mindful that they must reorganize or try a different strategy to take you out.

You can easily put someone off by saying something like, "I'll have to think about it," when they are trying to persuade you or get you to do anything. Normally, your manipulator wants you to act without thinking. Refusing to comply with their demands may agitate them a little and confuse them.

Another strategy for dealing with manipulation is to stay away from individuals or situations that give you anxiety. Remain away from someone you know is manipulating you until you manage to disregard their strategies or seize the initiative. If there are places where you feel uneasy and where people are pressuring you to do things against your will, avoid those places. Ignore them; it will make your life much less stressful. Trust your gut.

Taking responsibility or believing that they are flawed is one of the target's main problems. A manipulator wants precisely this. The moment you can maintain your composure and refuse to believe the lies the manipulator feeds you, you will have gained an advantage over them. You must stand back and have faith in yourself, regardless of what people say. Possess the optimism that displaces their negativity. Let their words and deeds pass by you without letting them sink in.

Considerations regarding your manipulator

They are essentially bullies most of the time.

Once you start to put your foot down, a manipulator will usually back down. They want easily controlled individuals who are docile and cooperative. When things get difficult, they'll probably give up.

Your manipulator frequently experiences victimization as well, and this is how they manage. That doesn't make it correct, but it might at least make it more considerate. Someone who is being abused or lacks control over their life is looking for their power. They look for someone they believe is weaker than themselves and go after them. They feel less exposed and more powerful as a result.

Sometimes, however, none of this is true; they are just manipulators in every way. Though you can't change them, you can dominate them and stop letting them rule you.

After assuming charge, you must establish limits. Setting limits is crucial, particularly for those you must often interact with. It is not an option for you to completely cut them out of your life. If so, it's crucial to maintain your boundaries and impose penalties on them when they cross them. This may cause people to reconsider you as weak by demonstrating your seriousness. However, maintain consistency. Similar to a child, your manipulator will continue to push the boundaries if you make a mistake even once.

Describe Manipulation.

Using your gestures, demeanour, hands, and even other body parts to manipulate someone or change a circumstance to suit your needs is known as manipulation. You may consider it self-serving, but I assure you that every transgression has a motivation. As a result, the motivation for manipulation may be advantageous. An example is when a skilled DJ tries to blend several musical genres to showcase his abilities in creating a beautiful sound mix for the audience. One could argue that this is nearly unjust to the song's original artist. Additionally, a skilled manipulator would know how to use words, emotions, and feelings to their advantage until their primary goal is achieved.

Manipulation may include a plan to control relationships and employing an indirect scheme. Telling a friend that they appear well when they are physically or mentally depressed is known as periodic manipulation. This is highly technical since it will impact how your friend sees you, ultimately impacting how they relate to you. Manipulation and emotional abuse are related, particularly when it occurs in intimate relationships. Depending on one's point of view, manipulation can be viewed negatively when the target of the manipulation experiences physical, emotional, or mental harm. On the other hand, some contend that manipulation subjugates and controls one's surroundings, including others. Furthermore, manipulation can negatively affect a person, and manipulators may struggle to connect with their true selves.

Understanding manipulation requires being able to distinguish between the three main kinds. The first type of choice manipulation involves changing the available options in the environment through rewards or threats. The second is information manipulation, in which a person's perspective is manipulated to the point where the issue is understood differently. Additionally, psychological manipulation is the act of influencing someone to alter their mental state of consciousness.

The hearer, motive, covertness, and speaker's interest are the four primary components of manipulations during manipulative encounters. Usually, these are called requirements for manipulation. The goal of manipulation is to influence a victim or hearer. Frequently, the target will act in a way that is contrary to how he acts before being tricked. When manipulation occurs, the manipulator's field of vision is wider than the target's, indicating that the manipulator is far more knowledgeable.

When it comes to motivation, is this not what makes manipulation what it is? The degree of manipulation of the target depends on the speaker's goal. The hearer must know this aim; otherwise, it would be counterproductive. Typically, there is communication between the speaker, the hearer, and the speaker's stated intentions.

Therefore, it must continue to be hidden for the general consensus on manipulation to hold. I can infer, pretty much, that one key component of manipulation is the speaker's motivation. It is made to fit the speaker's preferences and areas of interest. Additionally, I can inform you that a manipulator's motivation and mechanism of manipulation are related.

It is crucial to understand that while some people purposely manipulate, others manipulate subconsciously or without awareness. Manipulators with malicious intent are tricky. Because they are so conscious of what they do, they might even boast about it. Manipulators can be cunning, clever, and intelligent in manipulating. You cannot claim to be skilled at manipulating and caring about others when they are equally self-centred.

Neuro-Linguistic Programming Techniques

1. Anchorage: According to neurolinguistic programming, we continuously create an "anchor" between our emotional states and what we hear, see, and feel. Another name for this technique is classical conditioning. When a person experiences an emotion while exposed to a distinct stimulus (such as touch, sight, or sound), they typically establish an anchor—a link—between the stimulus and the feeling. The same emotional state is triggered if the same thing occurs again. According to neurolinguistic programming,

humans can consciously and purposefully design and activate triggers to assist them in reaching their desired states. Anxiety relief has been proven to be associated with the anchoring technique. Incorporating anchoring into NLP was inspired by family therapy and the Virginia Satir paradigm.

2. Pacing's future: Prospects Pacing is a strategy that involves having someone consider what they would like to do and then watch how they respond. This procedure is referred to as behavioural, cognitive, and feed-forward psychology. It's frequently employed to assess the effectiveness of the transformation process. For instance, if therapy and

medicine have eliminated or significantly reduced a person's dread or phobias. This is accomplished by watching a person's body language before and after surgery or therapy when they picture themselves in a challenging situation. The intervention has not been successful if the patient's body language does not change following the treatment.

A transition in the future-focused content can be inserted, seeded, and repaired using future pacing. This enables someone to experience handling a situation they would not have been able to handle well before they learned NLP. The goal of this simulation phase is to make the mind and brain incapable of distinguishing between a real-world scenario and a fictitious one.

According to the hypothesis, even though the previous scene was just imagined, having envisioned a situation and a favourable response can be a model for how to behave when a person experiences the event. Constructivism holds that the brain "accepts" such visions as fact and then makes a mental note of and shifts since it is thought that the brain cannot distinguish between imagination and truth, much as what happens to our dreams and reality. Put another way, the brain starts to take the scenario as fact and react to future events based on that "experience" or concept.

3. It suggests the patient must visualize a "trigger" that prompted them to engage in undesirable behaviour. For instance, a smoker's hand with a cigarette in it moves toward the face. Rather, the mind must be rewired to visualize a behaviour that will lead to the desired outcome, like stopping smoking. To begin with, you can quit smoking by seeing yourself as a fit, active, and healthy person. Swish's auditory effects are also employed to improve the user experience. It's a technique for neurolinguistic programming that involves submodality modulation.

4. It's reframing – Neurolinguistic programming is not the genesis of

reframing. This works by altering the interpretation of an occurrence, which alters the case's meaning. This is important because attitudes and reactions change along with the context. One can see the world differently and change the significance by reframing and employing words differently. Reframing occurs frequently in jokes, fairy tales, and sports. To begin with, in the story of the ugly duckling, after being embraced and acknowledged by the beautiful creatures, the duckling recognizes himself in the mirror and discovers that he is a swan as well.

4. Well-formed outcome: From the perspective of NLP, a well-formed

outcome is one of several "frames" in which the intended condition is seen as attainable and, if it is, productive. The patient defines a good outcome and outcome for their use and benefit. It is hoped that by allowing the patient to keep the beneficial outcomes of their unwanted conduct, the matter will be resolved in a way that is appropriate overall.

6. Ecology: Ecology is a framework that considers a patient's life and relationship from all aspects, weighing the intended outcome against the repercussions.

7. Integrating pieces: Parts integration is a kind of nonverbal communication predicated on the notion that disparate experiences and beliefs give rise to conflicting views about various facets of our lives and identities. In psychology, this is sometimes referred to as cognitive dissonance. Integrating the various facets of oneself by locating and negotiating with distinct parties to settle the internal conflict is known as the integration of parts. Family counselling and ego-state therapy arc two examples of this kind of NLP.

Chapter 3: NEURO LINGUISTIC PROGRAMMING PILLARS

It focuses on expert upgrades and is close to home. Since its introduction in the 1970s, natural language processing (NLP) has been seen as a revolutionary paradigm for human progress, using an extensive array of practical tools and findings from the field of brain science. Over the years, it has caused the monster to shift from precise restorative models to contextualized competent development forms. Basic concepts in self-awareness, such as eager insight, diverse knowledge hypotheses, sympathy, empathy, correspondence, and undivided attention, to name a few, are used to support this.

NLP started at the University of Santa Cruz in California in the middle of the 1970s. Dr John Grinder, a semantics educator, and Richard Bandler, an ace-level data sciences and math understudy, organized the event. Their focus was on those they considered to be exceptional communicators and advancement experts.

They identified four NLP pillars.

A foundational element is rapport. One of the most important gifts that NLP has given us is this. You must create compatibility when establishing relationships with others and yourself. NLP offers us amazing techniques for quickly establishing compatibility with others we manage to get along with.

Whether they are strangers or members of our own family, we may quickly and easily build affinity with them.

The second element is the awareness of the senses. The ability to perceive or feel things from our own five senses. When you walk into a person's house or another store, do you notice what you see—the colours and design—what you hear—music playing or people conversing—what you smell—food cooking—or what you see—flowers budding? We use our senses and perspectives to perceive the world around us. NLP helps us communicate more effectively by allowing us to realize how we perceive the world differently from how others would. Asking questions and seeing answers, or understanding how a person handles information, helps us better understand them and, as a result, improves communication with them.

Outcome thinking makes up the third pillar. This is related to focusing on what you need rather than what you don't. NLP provides tools to help you take charge of your life, focus on the desired outcomes, and achieve the necessary results. It motivates you to let go of unfavourable thoughts and beliefs and concentrate on desired goals.

Behavioural Flexibility is the fourth cornerstone. You should be flexible and adjust your behaviour if something isn't working. We gather a vast amount of data through the five detectors at every instant of the day. We are essentially unable to handle that much data at the conscious level. Therefore, the information we get is channelled by our mind into seven, give or take two, lumps that carry about 130 bits of information every second. What happens to the remaining data, then? We either summarize, manipulate, or delete it. We will all interpret the information differently since we have different worldviews based on our traits, beliefs, experiences, memories, and decisions.

NLP is presented as a craft and a study of correspondence, the path to knowledge and an exploration of your own and other people's priorities. It has also been portrayed as the path to achieving the desired results in all aspects of your life.

NLP has to do with increasing the range of options available to you. Developing relationships with people, practising focused, practical mindfulness, focusing more on outcomes, and honing your social skills can make you more capable than before and enable you to achieve your ideal goals and outcomes. In the unlikely event that you concentrate on it, everything is possible.

Objectives drive activities. NLP business preparation operates on the central tenet that when someone prioritizes a certain outcome, they become increasingly aware of the importance of completing their tasks. A sense of conscious intention is fundamental and is achieved using several flexible methods.

Let's use a model to understand these. You must learn how to paddle a boat. The outcome you are examining is shipping the vessel from one coast to the other shore. Paddling starts, and you become aware of your course—a palpable sharpness. You compare it to where you ought to go, and if you discover that you are not on the right track, you change your direction (adaptability). This cycle would be repeated until you reach the opposite shore (result).

To demonstrate how these NLP columns apply, you may also extend their use to any situation about business. Later, we'll examine how these concepts are applied to work and commercial situations. I would mostly focus on explaining the technical details in the first few posts.

Why is learning NLP necessary for a person?

NLP was created by modelling, who was incredibly talented in the therapeutic field. It is the application of workable methods and strategies to modify your thinking and communication to achieve remarkable and improved results. Many industries use NLP systems and models, including training, business, sport, education, health, and social and self-awareness.

Many people study NLP to become brave. Confidence blossoms, and NLP teaches you how to feel good about yourself from the inside out when you learn to like who you are. Release any internalized anxiousness and quickly alter your mood. You may offer yourself clarity when you need it by utilizing NLP. Many people use these crucial tools to help them become exceptional public speakers.

Many people ask themselves, "Would it be a good idea for me to learn NLP?" when they first hear about the field.

What possible advantages does this have for me?

Will I find use for it in the future?

There are numerous suitable answers. People typically study Neuro-Linguistic Programming, or NLP, since it provides them with the tools and experiences to...

Feel more responsible for their thoughts and perspectives

Make your communication even more effective and convincing.

They should grow personally and acquire the tools necessary to live more fulfilling lives.

How Should Your Goals Be Formulated?

This is a crucial question asking whether neuro-linguistic programming is practical and effective. It will be challenging for us to decide on a goal. To become a skilled NLP practitioner, we must first learn how to do it successfully; otherwise, it will be challenging for us to extend it regularly. This field also provides us with a straightforward formula for creating precise and, most importantly, successful objectives.

We might establish several requirements to ensure our objective is reachable. Its concreteness—you have to be specific about what you want—is one of them. For instance, deciding that finding a new job is your objective is insufficient. You must be very specific about the type of job you want, the department you want to work in, the way you want to advance in it, the time you want to work on it, and the location for your objective to be definite and, thus, more likely to be achieved. Here, accuracy is crucial. An objective statement such as "I am looking for a job that meets my financial expectations and in which I can develop" is a better way to state your desired outcome than saying, "I do not want to work in this place." I wish to change jobs because of this.

The time frame by which you want to accomplish your goal must be precise; it cannot be "in the future"; it must be, for example, April of this year. It's important to consider how you will determine whether your objective has been fully accomplished. Imagine reaching your objective in your mind's eye. What does it look like? Which senses are involved? What noises are you aware of? What observations do you have? How are you going to feel on the inside right now? Give it some thought. The objective must also be ecological, meaning it should not hurt anyone but benefit you and the environment. To achieve your objective, you must modify its ecosystem to fit the circumstances and consider how things might change along the way. For instance, is switching to a career with demanding deadlines that would sever your relationships with your loved ones worthwhile? How will this impact your mental health and how you handle stress? Are you going to be successful? It is insufficient to just contemplate your objective; to accomplish it, put it in writing and periodically review the precise words you used. This will help you stay focused on the objective and help you remember what's important.

Once a deadline has been established, break up the time allotted for execution into smaller windows, during which you will allocate distinct jobs. Smaller goals are simpler for us to accomplish than larger ones, and they also enable us to monitor our efficacy and motivation, which rise as we take little, efficient steps from a predetermined list that move us closer to our objectives and demonstrate the usefulness of our strategy. Now is the time to start putting your goal down in writing. Making a list of the items and tasks that are most important will undoubtedly help you stay motivated and productive when doing other duties. Don't put off starting this task; the sooner you do so, the better. Don't allow your objectives and aspirations to remain unreal, unreachable fantasies. Allow your aspirations for objectives to start materializing; careful goal-setting and preparation will undoubtedly assist you. Now, take out a piece of paper and begin to write. I wish you luck in being successful!

www.ingramcontent.com/pod-product-compliance
Lightning Source LLC
Chambersburg PA
CBHW052137110526
44591CB00012B/1755